THE JUMP ROPE BOOK

Glen Vecchione

Illustrated by Jason Hurst

Sterling Publishing Co., Inc.   New York

ACKNOWLEDGMENTS:

Many thanks to California and Indiana contacts Amy Steward and Lee Stienbarger, Cliff Bogdan in Canada, Roger Smithies in the U.K., and both Greg Bannerman and Cameron Prout in Australia. May their Olympic dreams come true!

Also, heartfelt thanks to Jason Hurst for his capable illustrations, and to my editor, Sheila Anne Barry, for putting it all together.

Library of Congress Cataloging-in-Publication Data

Vecchione, Glen.
    The jump rope book / Glen Vecchione ; illustrated by Jason Hurst.
        p.   cm.
    Includes index.
    ISBN 0-8069-0682-0
    1. Rope skipping. I. Title.
GV498.V43   1995
796.2—dc20

                                   94-48171
                                       CIP

10 9 8 7 6 5 4 3 2 1
First paperback edition published in 1996 by
Sterling Publishing Company, Inc.
387 Park Avenue South, New York, N.Y. 10016
© 1995 by Glen Vecchione
Distributed in Canada by Sterling Publishing
% Canadian Manda Group, One Atlantic Avenue, Suite 105
Toronto, Ontario, Canada M6K 3E7
Distributed in Great Britain and Europe by Cassell PLC
Wellington House, 125 Strand, London WC2R 0BB, England
Distributed in Australia by Capricorn Link (Australia) Pty Ltd.
P.O. Box 6651, Baulkham Hills, Business Centre, NSW 2153, Australia
Manufactured in the United States of America
All rights reserved

Sterling ISBN 0-8069-0682-0 Trade
             0-8069-0683-9 Paper

Contents

Although jumping rope can provide healthful exercise for just about everyone, you need to observe a few precautions. Always get a clean bill of health from your doctor before beginning any new exercise, even if you exercise regularly.

Before You Begin

No one knows the name of the first person who paused from twirling hemp into rope and began twirling rope for fun. Unlike the toys of Archimedes, Leonardo da Vinci, and the venerable Thomas Edison, the details of the original jump rope were never recorded. And why would they be? Nothing was more commonplace than *corde, Tau,* rope—an everyday object used for everything from hanging clothes to hanging thieves.

But we do know that people jumped rope as far back as ancient Egypt—and all over the world. In Sweden, stiff wicker was used; in Hungary, plaited straw. Spanish children used leather thongs, while French children jumped over fancy ropes woven on spool looms. In England, the children of mill workers had handles made from wooden bobbin spindles. Native Americans jumped using twisted grapevines, and in American cities, the kids on the block grabbed anything from window sash cord to crate twine. Everyone jumped, and the jumping continues!

For good reason. Jumping rope stimulates your mind as well as your muscles. It sharpens your reflexes and improves your coordination. It helps you get comfortable with the movement of your body so that you develop grace and style, as well as strength and endurance. And, it's fun.

Jumping rope requires little space and less time. Performed every other day, even simple stepping routines help you to lose weight. Like swimming and skiing, vigorous jumping involves the whole body—ankles, knees, waist, shoulders, arms, and wrists all move together for total aerobic conditioning.

In these pages you will find a wide variety of rope activities: jumping alone, jumping with a partner, and jumping in teams. You'll also discover things to do with a rope when you *don't* feel like jumping, like fancy twirling tricks or isometric exercises using a looped rope.

You'll start with the basics, such as what kind of rope works best for you, what to wear, and how to warm up. There's a routine for everyone here: "stepping" for the exercise-shy couch potato or active senior, "tiny kicks" for the more adventurous jumper, and "pretzels" for the lean, mean, exercise machine. On pages 60–61 you'll find a list of all the routines according to their level of difficulty. By checking this list, you'll see at a glance whether a routine is right for you.

For the serious jumper, there's up-to-date information about competitions and the organizations that sponsor them. The less intense will find fun rhymes to keep them going. And we've provided a suggested playlist of both classical and popular music that makes jumping extra enjoyable.

So what are you waiting for? Clear off a place on your patio or living-room floor and *start jumping!*

CHAPTER 1
Getting Started
•••••••••••••••••••••••••••••••

CHOOSING A ROPE AND OTHER BASICS

Before you begin, you'll need to find a rope that suits your height, strength, skill level, and expectations. You'll also need the right kind of shoes and a good surface to jump on. If you prepare properly, you'll learn basic techniques quickly and have fun at the same time. You'll also reduce the risk of sprains and other injuries, particularly if you aren't used to jumping.

Take some time to choose your rope. Toy stores, novelty stores, and sporting goods shops carry a large variety of ropes. These range from simple, woven ropes (best for beginners) to ropes made from soft plastic beads. Since even the finest ropes rarely cost very much, you can start with a simple rope and replace it with a more elaborate one as you improve.

You can also make your own jump rope from a strong piece of cotton clothesline, but make sure you give it handles. You can make them by attaching two four-inch-long sections of narrow PVC pipe to the ends of the rope. Knot the rope on both sides of each section. The rope should turn freely within the handles.

■ Rope Length

The length of your rope depends on your height. If the rope is too short, you end up with poor jumping posture, making it difficult to be accurate, especially in the more complex routines. If the rope is too long, it can bounce up and hit your ankles, causing you to trip. The right length ensures speed, grace, and precision.

Check to see if a rope is the right length for you by placing one foot in the middle of the rope and lifting both ends up to your chest. The handles should just reach your armpits.

If a rope is too short, there isn't much you can do except replace it with a longer one. But you can shorten a rope that's too long by tying one or more knots in it. Tie the knots several inches from the ends. Try to maintain a balanced rope weight. If your rope needs two knots, tie one at one end and the other at the other end. However, if your rope requires more than four knots, you might consider replacing it with a shorter rope.

Licorice ropes, made from lightweight vinyl plastic, resemble licorice strands. These ropes cost very little and work well for high-speed jumping. They have very little drag and cut cleanly through the air.

Weighted ropes guarantee a good workout, and some can help you achieve a solid, graceful jumping technique as well. The extra weight is in the rope handles or in the rope itself. The amount of weight varies from one-third of a pound to five pounds (.15kg to 2.25kg). It's a good idea to avoid trying anything fancy with a weighted rope, and make sure you're in good physical condition before even attempting to use one.

▪ Jump Rope Checklist

Before you buy a rope, make sure the handles are comfortable in your hands. Check to see if the rope pivots freely within the handles. Tight handles cause a rope to twist, increasing the danger of tripping. Avoid ropes that stretch when you pull a section between your hands. At high speeds, ropes stretch too much and can confuse even skilled jumpers.

▪ Types of Rope

Simple woven ropes of cotton, nylon, or polypropylene are best for beginning jumpers. Woven ropes create more "drag," or air resistance, as they rotate, so they're not as useful for high-speed jumping. But they are good for warm-ups and for practicing basic jumping techniques. The softer quality of a woven rope ensures less of a sting when the rope hits you, and it will!

Several other types of rope, some specifically designed for speed and for fancy routine work, are available. The beaded rope is good for speed and fancy routine work. It has short, cylindrical, plastic beads strung over a nylon cord. The advantage of a beaded rope is its added weight and stability. It won't tangle easily during a complicated routine. Because of the weight of the beads, wind is less of a factor when you jump outside. Some of these segmented ropes feature adjustable lengths. You can add or subtract beads to suit your height.

▪ What to Wear

Never jump barefoot. You need to wear shoes that will protect your feet from repetitive impact motion. A good pair of athletic shoes will support your ankles and cushion the balls of your feet. Make sure your shoes fit snugly.

▪ Where to Jump

Always jump on a solid surface. This will lessen the risk of sprain injuries, particularly if you haven't been jumping very much.

So now you have your shoes and the perfect jump rope and can't wait to begin. You're almost ready, but first you need to do some warm-up exercises to loosen your joints and get your blood going!

WARM-UP EXERCISES

Jumping rope involves your entire body, from top to bottom. Your shoulders, waist, wrists, knees, and ankles all need loosening up before you begin. The following exercises prepare your body for the repetitive impact motion that is an essential part of good jumping technique.

▪ Shoulder Rolls

Stand with your arms at your sides, feet apart, knees slightly bent. Hunch your shoulders forward and make a slow rolling motion, tracing a circle with your shoulders. Make five circles, then reverse direction.

▪ Jackknife Stretch

Stand with your arms at your sides, feet close together, knees slightly bent. Keep your posture as straight as possible. Slowly raise your right knee until you can grasp your leg with both hands. Hold your leg just below the knee and pull it up towards your chest as high as you can without feeling uncomfortable. Slowly lower your knee to the starting position. Repeat the stretch with the left knee. Do a total of five stretches for each knee, alternating knees.

■ Single Jump

Stand with your arms at your sides, feet slightly apart, knees slightly bent. Practice jumping on the balls of your feet. Don't let your heels touch the ground. If you find this tiring after a while, you may touch your heels to the ground every few jumps, but remember that the graceful bounce of a good jumper comes from mastering the technique of jumping on the balls of the feet. Continue jumping for one minute.

■ Double Jump

When you jump at a moderate speed, a balancing bounce often occurs between the times you actually jump over the rope. This bounce is smaller than a jump. It helps to stabilize you and prepare you for the real jump. It also adds a pleasing rhythm to your jumping routine. You can practice by alternating jumps with bounces. For a little variety, try jumping with your feet apart and bouncing with your feet together. You can also jump on one foot, alternating feet with each jump.

■ Turning the Rope

Now add a rope to your warm-up exercises to improve your coordination, but in this exercise, turn the rope in one hand only. Jumping over it comes later.

Hold both ends of the rope in your right hand. To start turning, swing the rope overhead from your back. Your right shoulder and lower arm should make a full circle. Keep the rope in motion by concentrating movement in your wrist. Your elbow stays close to your body, your arm stretches slightly outward, and your hand is just under your waist. Propel the rope forward by wrist action alone, your hand making small circles with the rope, while your arm hardly moves. Allow the rope to crack solidly against the ground. Listen to the rhythm. After two minutes, switch hands and repeat the exercise.

■ Static Jumps

Hold the handles of the rope securely. Keep your arms against your sides. Step over the rope so that your first turn is back-to-front. It will bolster your confidence when you see the rope moving towards your feet.

Turn the rope overhead, using your shoulders and lower arms. Jump with both feet, just high enough so that the rope passes under you and hits the ground with a pleasing *crack*. Stop and think about the movement. If you missed the rope by jumping too soon or too late, or if your feet didn't leave the ground at the same time and became tangled, try again. It won't take long before your eyes, mind, and body all work together.

After you master the back-to-front jump, reverse direction. You need to get a feel for the rope as it approaches you from behind. Again, stop and think about what you did right or wrong. Reverse jumping may seem difficult at first, but it will get easier, and the split-second timing it requires actually improves your overall jumping skill.

■ Jumping Rope

Now it's time to put it all together. Relax, take a deep breath, and try to remember everything you've learned so far. Hold the ends of the rope, turn it overhead from the back, and *jump!* Take a small balancing bounce as the rope passes over your head and *jump again!* Listen to the rhythmic *crack* of the rope and feel your body dancing to the rhythm. The fun has just begun.

Before learning the fancier steps, you need to practice basic jumping whenever you can. If you can jump 20 times at a moderate speed without missing, start increasing your speed. Remember to jump on the balls of your feet as much as you can.

WORDS AND MUSIC

Simple solo jumping takes on a whole new dimension when you combine it with rhymes or music. Chanting a rhyme while jumping, or jumping to the right kind of music, will help you relax and stabilize your jumping rhythm. Also, many rhymes will keep you going for at least 20 turns, so you don't have to bother counting.

Jump rope rhymes have been around a long time, and many of the following may be familiar to you.

Abraham-a-Lincoln never was a crook
And that's because his nose was always in a book.
So how many books did he read each day?
Don't ask me, 'cause I really couldn't say.

Abraham-a-Lincoln always said his prayers,
But he made his father angry by jumping off the
        chairs.
He had to walk to school in the deep, cold snow.
So how many miles did poor Abe go—?
1, 2, 3, 4, 5, etc.

In this example, it takes 32 jumps (four jumps per line) to get through the rhyming part. The counting part at the end allows you to continue jumping as long as you want.

Other rhymes end with counting lines, too. In some of these, the jumper might eventually trip at some point while counting; in others, the last number counted has some special meaning. Here are a few examples:

I love to jump upon my bed or roll along the
        ground.
I love the way the jumping rope goes 'round and
        'round and 'round.

But if I trip and bang my head I don't know what
    I'd do.
I'd surely get a great big lump and maybe even two.

So how many big lumps will I get—?
1, 2, 3, 4, 5, etc.

My father caught a quail.
He put it in a pail.
He brought it home to mother,
Who pulled it by the tail.

She said, "It breaks my heart.
A quail just isn't smart.
I'd rather buy a chicken at the local grocery mart."

So how many chickens did she buy—?
1, 2, 3, 4, 5, etc.

Alphabet rhymes also tease and challenge the jumper.

Yellow as a pancake, white as a dove,
Tell me the name of the person I'll love.
A, B, C, D, E, etc.

Tiny as a bee stinger, big as a tree,
Tell me the name of the one who loves me.
Z, Y, X, W, etc.

If you make it through the alphabet once, you can go
through again, starting from the beginning or end, as you
like.

If you jump with a friend, you can take turns reciting
the same rhyme to see who can jump longer.

Some of these rhymes can be chanted by a second person so that the jumper can follow the instructions in the
rhyme.

Policeman, policeman, stop that thief!
Then make him jump without relief.
Make him jump and kick his feet,
Make him jump until he's beat!
Make him jump and tap his nose,
Make him jump and click his toes,
And when it's almost time for supper,
Make him jump like *red hot pepper!*

"Red hot pepper" tells the jumper to turn the rope as fast as possible and to jump until tired or until the chanter starts the rhyme again at a moderate speed.

Of course, you can make up rhymes to suit the occasion or to fit the personalities of the jumpers. Rhyming makes practicing fun, and the more you practice, the sooner you advance.

Choosing music requires some care and patience. You'll want something lively but with a moderate tempo and pronounced beat. Avoid music that slows down or speeds up too much. Music in triple time (¾) poses complications since you jump in double time—that is, one over-the-rope jump and one balancing hop. If you try jumping to a waltz, for instance, you'll find the rhythmic emphasis shifting from the jump to the hop, then back again. Jumping to music should be fun and effortless. You want to avoid counting as much as possible.

Some classical pieces are real "foot-tappers" and make for terrific jumping. It's fun, exciting, and at the same time wonderfully relaxing to jump to the likes of Mozart or Bach. They certainly add a touch of elegance to acrobatic techniques. Also the length of classical pieces makes them ideal for elaborate jumping routines, but if you like shorter, more intense musical accompaniment, stick to pop tunes. Some suggestions for each follow.

Classical Pieces

J.S. Bach	*Brandenburg* Concerto no. 3, first movement
	Brandenburg Concerto no. 6, first movement
	Brandenburg Concerto no. 2, second movement
Vivaldi	*The Four Seasons*, "Spring" Concerto for Two Violins in A minor, op. 3 (RV. 522), no. 8, first movement
Mozart	"*Eine Kleine Nachtmusik*," first movement

Popular Songs

"Papa Don't Preach"	Madonna
"The Locomotion"	Kylie Minogue
"New Attitude"	Patti LaBelle
"Thriller"	Michael Jackson
"Uptown Girl"	Billy Joel
"Chapel of Love"	The Dixiecups
"Summer Nights"	Olivia Newton John
"Gonna Make You Sweat"	C & C Music Factory
"California Girls"	The Beach Boys

It's best to avoid wearing portable cassettes or CD players while you jump; they can slip off and distract you.

When you've mastered the basic solo jump and can do it with grace, ease, and confidence, you're ready to move on to the solo routines in the following chapter. If you're still a little unsteady on your feet, remember: practice makes perfect. *Keep jumping!*

CHAPTER 2
Solo Jumping

●●●●●●●●●●●●●●●●●●●●●●●●●●

BACK TO THE FUTURE

You might call the routines in the next two chapters the "classics" of jump rope. They have passed down from one generation of jumpers to another with few, if any, changes. Although we've renamed a few like The Skier and Judo Jump, the basic movements were once part of every jumper's repertoire.

Who invented these routines? No one in particular, and everyone. Or to put it another way: they are part of the same folklore that produced rhymes and songs, street games, and tall tales. Maybe they've survived so long because they're all relatively easy and lots of fun. No matter. Mastering the "old standards" will also prepare you for fancier jumping. And, as rope jumping continues to evolve into a serious, competitive sport, they will help to groom you to participate in an ever-widening global network of contests.

FANCY FOOTWORK

The following routines emphasize movement in the feet and lower legs. In most cases, the fancy footwork occurs during the balancing bounce, so you won't have to worry about clearing the rope while concentrating on a new foot position. You can create an advanced version of some routines by leaving out the balancing bounce between each new position.

Before learning a new routine, draw or imagine a horizontal line running beneath your feet. The line will keep you centered and allow you to focus your movements so that they remain tight and clean.

Always warm up before starting a routine. Start your warm-up period with the exercises described earlier and finish with 20 basic feet-together jumps.

■ Heel Tap

For the first turn, jump over the rope with feet together. Take a balancing bounce as the rope passes overhead.

On the second turn, begin your jump with feet together, but land so that your left foot is on the line. At the same time, tap your right heel in front of the line.

Keep your feet together for the next balancing bounce; then begin the third jump with feet together, but land with your right foot *on* the line and your left heel in front of it.

If you leave out the feet-together jumps, you've mastered the next routine.

■ Keep On Truckin'

Take the first jump with your feet together. From then on, reverse the position of your feet, as before, with every

turn of the rope. Lean back slightly and turn the upper half of your body from side to side with each jump. Start slowly, then gradually increase your speed. You can actually walk around the room with this one!

■ Toe Tap

Begin by jumping with both feet together.

The next turn, begin your jump with feet together, but land so that your left foot is on the line. At the same time, tap your right toe on the ground behind the line.

Reverse positions for the following turn, and so on.

■ The Charlie Chaplin

Combining the heel tap with the toe tap creates a funny walk that may remind you of the way Chaplin moved in the silent movies.

Begin by jumping with both feet together.

The second turn, land so that your left foot is on the line, tapping your right heel in front of the line.

The third turn, jump so that your left foot is on the line. At the same time, tap your right toe on the ground behind the line.

■ Heel Click (Buck and Wing)

Practice this routine without the rope first. Hop twice with your right foot, then twice with your left foot. When you have a good, solid hop, you are ready to add the click and the rope.

The first turn, hop on your right foot while moving your left foot towards the right and lifting it about six inches (15cm) from the ground.

After you land, as the rope passes overhead, push off with your right foot and click your heels to the left. Land on your left foot with your right foot lifted six inches (15 cm) from the ground and reverse the sequence.

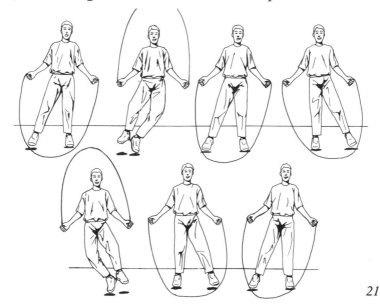

■ The Side Step

Turn your body so that the baseline runs vertically—between your feet, not under them. Jump with both feet together for the first turn. Take the balancing bounce with your left foot. At the same time, tap your right toe out to the side.

The second turn, jump with your feet together again. Take the next balancing bounce with your right foot, as you tap your left toe out to the side.

The third turn, jump with your feet together, and so on.

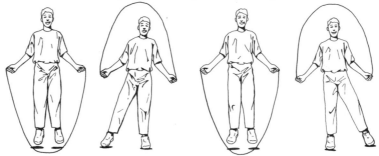

■ Right and Left Crisscross

Begin by jumping with both feet together. For the balancing bounce, cross your right leg in front of your left leg at the knee. Be prepared to jump over the second turn of the rope with both feet together again. The next balancing bounce, cross your left leg in front of your right leg.

Place your feet together for the third turn.

A more advanced version of the Crisscross requires that you jump over the rope and land in the crisscross position, alternating a right cross with a left cross. Only attempt this after you have practiced crisscrossing between jumps. Crisscrossing can be rough on unprepared ankles.

■ The Scissors Step

This step, also called a Bleke, requires your feet to alternate front and back positions for each balancing bounce between jumps. In this routine, you may leave out the feet-together jumps, but go slowly.

The following routines leave out the balancing bounce between jumps. Start slowly, paying attention to balance, coordination, and good jumping form.

■ Running in Place

On the first turn of the rope, jump with both feet together.

On the second turn, jump with your right foot. Keep your left foot a little behind and raised, so that it doesn't touch the rope.

On the third turn, reverse the position of your feet so that you raise your right foot, while jumping with your left foot.

As you increase the speed of your rope, you'll find yourself running in place. Try this with music.

■ Tiny Kicks

Jump over the rope with both feet, but land on the ball of your right foot. As the rope passes overhead, take a balancing hop with your right foot and kick your left foot out in front of you.

The second turn of the rope, jump with both feet, but land on the ball of your left foot. As the rope passes overhead, take a balancing hop with your left foot, while kicking your right foot out in front of you.

Keep the movement small and concentrated and don't try to jump too fast. Work on your balance and try to create a graceful, dancelike movement.

Remember, you take no balancing bounces between jumps in these routines. Listen for the rhythm of the jump in the movement of your feet. If you practice each day, these routines will sharpen the coordination between your eyes, mind and body.

The following routines combine whimsy with good form. Feel free to improvise.

■ Twister

Take the first jump with both feet together.

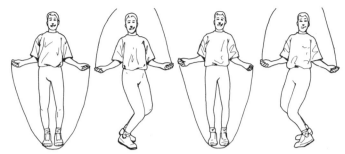

The second jump, keep your legs together and twist at the waist, keeping your chest forward. Face forward and jump with your feet together for the third jump.

Twist in the opposite direction for the fourth jump.

■ The Can-Can

Make sure you warm up with a few Tiny Kicks before attempting these high kicks.

Kick out straight and high between feet-together jumps. Don't push for speed, instead concentrate on good, solid jumping. The perfect Can-Can musical accompaniment is Offenbach's *Gaîté Parisienne*.

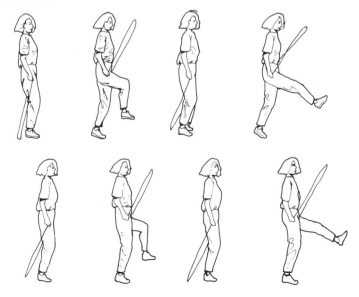

Give yourself a few weeks to master these routines, always warming up before you start practicing. As you grow more confident in your ability to do several things with your feet while jumping, you'll want to involve the rest of your body.

GETTING PHYSICAL

After you learn some of the basic footwork and gain confidence in your ability to maintain form and speed, you'll want your jumping to become a little more physically challenging. Although even simple jumping provides good exercise, the following routines go a little further, involving more leg, waist, chest, and arm muscles.

Don't become discouraged if a routine seems too difficult at first. Take each one slowly, concentrating on coordinating the movements. Remember to draw your horizontal baseline; it's particularly important for many of these routines. You might want to try practicing without the rope first. Soon, even the most demanding set of movements will seem like second nature to you.

Never start a practice session without first warming up. Shoulder Rolls and Jackknife Stretches will loosen your muscles, increase your circulation, and reduce the risk of sprains.

■ The Skier

Turn your body so that you straddle the baseline. Take the first jump with both feet together. For the balancing bounce, keep your feet together and jump to the right of the line.

Take the second jump with both feet together straddling the line, and the next balancing bounce with both feet to the left of the line.

Try to keep your legs straight as you bounce from one side of the line to the other between jumps.

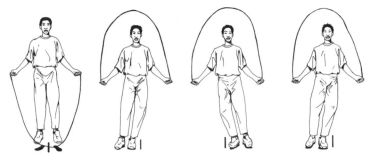

A more challenging version of The Skier leaves out the straddling jumps. You jump over the rope as you move from one side of the line to the other.

■ Jumping Jacks

Turning this familiar exercise into a jump-rope routine makes it much more vigorous and enjoyable.

Begin with your feet straddling the baseline. Jump over the first turn of the rope with both feet together.

Jump over the second turn of rope with your feet apart.

Take the third turn with your feet together, and so on. No balancing bounces are allowed.

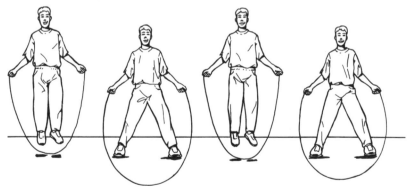

■ Jumping-Jack Scissors-Step Combination

As the name implies, this routine combines the plain Jumping Jack with the Scissors Step you read about on page 23.

The Scissors Step comes between jumps (see page 28).

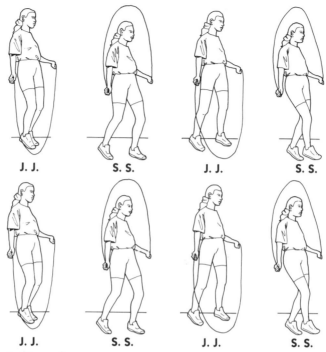

J. J.   S. S.   J. J.   S. S.

J. J.   S. S.   J. J.   S. S.

■ High Stepping

Your hamstrings get a good workout with this routine. Try it slowly and increase your speed gradually.

Jump over the first turn of the rope with your feet together.

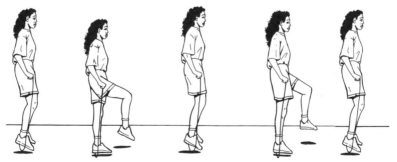

The second turn, jump with your right foot, while lifting your left knee as high as possible.

Jump with your feet together on the third turn. On the

fourth turn, jump with your left foot, lifting your right knee as high as possible.

For a particularly robust version of this routine, go from foot to foot for each jump, as if you were climbing a huge staircase.

■ Bullfighter

In this routine, your arms will welcome the chance to move about a little more than in previous routines.

Begin by swinging the rope with both hands to your right side. Bend your knees a little as you swing. As the rope swings above you, separate your hands so that the rope opens as it approaches the ground. Jump over the rope with your feet close together.

As the rope swings above you a second time, pull your hands together to close the rope, bringing it down on your left side.

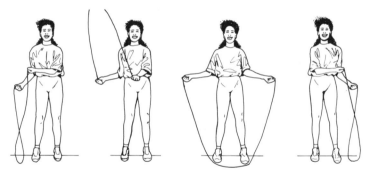

■ Front Cross

This routine will impress your friends, particularly when you learn to combine it with other routines using the arms. You might want to try the movements without the rope first.

Hold your arms out from the sides of your body a little farther than usual. Bend them only slightly. Turn the rope, concentrating the motion more in the shoulders than the wrists. As your rope approaches its highest point, begin crossing your arms so that they overlap at the forearms. By the time the rope reaches your feet again, your arms should be crossed broadly enough so that you can jump over the looped rope.

Now begin uncrossing your arms as the rope approaches its second zenith. By the time it reaches your feet, the rope is unlooped and easily jumped.

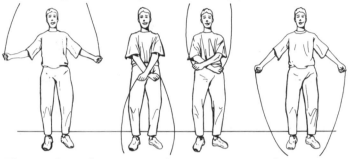

The trick to this routine lies in crossing the arms widely enough to make a loop that is large enough to jump through. You must also take care to cross your arms equally, so that one forearm doesn't stick out more than the other forearm, ruining your loop.

■ Half Round

Face forward and take the first jump with both feet together.

As the rope passes its zenith and begins to come down, keep your arms straight but turn your body a quarter of the way to the right, so that you take the second jump at a bit of an angle.

Turn your body another quarter to the right, taking the third jump at even more of an angle.

Come back, so that you are facing forward again, on the fourth jump. You are actually taking quarter turns to the left with each jump. The challenge here is keeping your arm position constant as you twist your body. The rope should pass under you, as if you were still jumping face forward.

■ Around the World

It might seem easy, but this routine takes a little practice if you want it to look right. Take the first jump with your feet together.

Make a full body quarter turn with each subsequent jump, until you make a complete circle. Unlike the Half Round, in this routine your arms rotate with your body. The tricky part is that the rope, suddenly forced to change direction in mid-spin, becomes wobbly and hard to control. This presents a real technical challenge.

■ Touch Jumps

The basic motion of this routine consists of stepping forward and back.

Stand on the baseline. Take the first jump with your right foot.

Step forward and take the second jump in front of the line with your left foot. At the same time, bend your right leg at the knee and touch the right heel to the back of the left knee.

The third jump, reverse the sequence. Step back with your right foot and touch your left heel to the back of your right knee.

Now that you understand how jumping rope can involve the whole body—and what's more, now that your *body* understands it—it's important to practice until you can execute the routines fearlessly. The next section will combine much of what you've learned so far in new and exciting ways.

ADVANCED TECHNIQUES

Once you've reached a certain level of speed and power in your jumping, you're ready to work on the clarity and precision that these new techniques require. Mastering them will make you a truly impressive solo jumper.

■ Right and Left Turn Hops

A one-legged version of the Around the World routine in the previous section, Right and Left Turn Hops really puts your balance to the test.

Take the first jump with both feet together.

Hop with the right foot for the following jumps, making a quarter turn clockwise until you've traced a full circle.

Now switch to the left foot and make quarter turns counterclockwise until you've traced another full circle.

■ One-Leg Sideways Jump

Warm up for this routine by doing a few Left and Right Crisscross jumps. Draw, or imagine, a line stretching between your feet.

Take the first turn with both feet together.

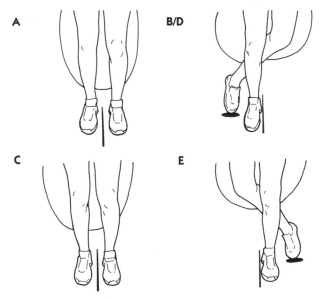

For the second turn, take a sideways jump with both feet together, landing so that the ball of your right foot comes down slightly to the right of the line. At the same time, bend your left leg at the knee, cross it behind your right leg, and touch the ground with your toe. This results in a jaunty, dancelike movement.

Take the third turn with both feet together. On the fourth turn, jump sideways in the opposite direction.

■ Road Runner

Jump with both feet together for the first turn of the rope.

Begin the second jump with both feet together, but once in the air, flip the right lower leg forward and the left lower leg backwards. Keep your knees together.

Take a balancing bounce with feet together, if necessary, then reverse leg positions for the third turn of the rope.

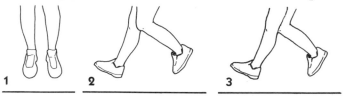

■ Heels Out–Heels In

Take the first jump with both feet together.

Begin the second jump with both feet together, but land on the balls of your feet so that your toes turn in and your heels turn out. Your knees should touch.

Begin the third jump with both feet together, but land on your heels while turning out your toes. Bend your knees slightly outward.

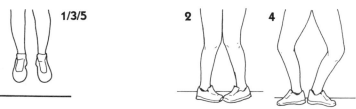

■ Rocker

To help you master this routine, feel free to take balancing bounces between jumps.

Draw, or imagine, a horizontal line stretching beneath your feet. Stand on the line and take the first turn with both feet together.

For the second turn, lean slightly forward at the waist, and jump so that your right foot lands in front of the line. At the same time, extend the left leg backwards.

For the third turn, kick forward with your left foot so that it lands near the spot vacated by your right foot. As you kick, extend your right leg forward above the floor. Lean backwards with your head and shoulders.

For the fourth turn, lean slightly forward at the waist again, and kick backwards with your right foot so that it lands near the spot vacated by your left foot. Extend your left leg backwards.

■ Judo Jump

This routine is a lot like the Scissors Step, but the movements are bolder and the effect more powerful.

Take the first jump with both feet together.

Begin the second jump with your feet together, but land in a slight crouch with your right foot forward and your left foot backwards. Spread your feet apart as wide as you can without discomfort.

As the rope passes overhead, stand up straight and take

a balancing bounce with both feet together. Begin the third jump with both feet together, but land in a crouch with your left foot forward and your right foot backwards. Again, spread your feet far apart.

■ Behind the Back Cross

This is an impressive routine, particularly when combined with other crossing routines.

The first turn of the rope, jump with both feet together. As soon as you finish the jump, bring your hands behind your back and start crossing your arms. As the rope approaches its zenith—its highest point—cross your arms as tightly as possible, so that your hands stick out at your sides at waist level. Your hands should stick out far enough so that the loop of the rope is wide enough to pass over your body as it comes back down towards your feet.

Keeping your arms crossed, jump over the rope again. As it passes behind you and begins to climb, quickly uncross your arms so that you're back in your original position for the following jump.

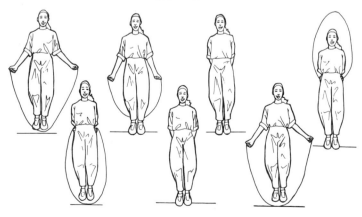

■ Front to Back Cross

The first turn of the rope, jump with both feet together. As the rope passes overhead, bring your left hand across to your right side. As soon as the rope closes and hits the ground, bring your right hand behind your back so that it crosses to your left side.

Keep your hands in this front-to-back cross position with your hands sticking out far enough so that the rope can pass over and under you. After you've jumped again, exit the cross position by simply bringing your arms back to your sides. The rope will return to its original position.

■ Bent Over

You can "walk" your way through this routine until you feel comfortable with the unusual positions. Much of what you've learned so far comes together here, including reverse turning.

Take the first jump with both feet together, but land with your feet apart. As the rope passes overhead and comes forward, bring your hands together and bend at the waist. The rope passes between your legs. With your hands now behind your legs, immediately cross your arms. Extend them as far as possible—right hand behind the left leg and left hand behind the right leg—so that the rope opens up and passes over you.

Remaining in this bent-over position, allow the rope to pass over your back and head. The rope stops when it lands on the ground.

Jump or step over the rope, raise your hands, and bring them forward through your legs. Open your hands, and you'll find yourself in the original jumping position, ready to do the whole routine again!

■ Pretzel

Mastering this routine will make you a hero to your jump-rope friends. Again, "walk" through it carefully to master the positions before actually attempting to jump.

Take the first jump with both feet together.

The second turn of the rope, hop with your left foot. At

the same time, lift your right knee up behind your arm.

Hop in this position for the third turn. As soon as the rope passes under your left foot, move your right hand behind your right knee. You've become a pretzel!

Hold this position and hop on your left foot for a few turns of the rope.

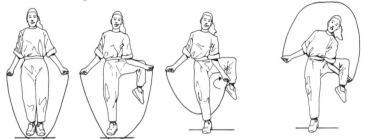

To exit the Pretzel, instead of hopping over the rope with your left foot, bring your right hand from under your knee to meet your left hand as the rope approaches the ground. The rope closes and swings to the side. When the rope passes over your left shoulder, bring your right hand back to your right side.

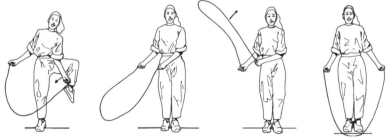

Now you've returned to your original jumping position. Jump with your feet together for the next few turns and do it again.

■ Double-and-Triple Under

You don't have to stretch into any unusual positions for this routine, but don't be fooled. Well-executed Double-and-Triple Unders challenge even the most accomplished jumpers.

Turn the rope two or three times between jumps. Obviously, you must turn the rope very quickly. Intersperse your Double or Triple Unders with single jumps to give yourself some breathing room. Though turning the rope more than once requires stamina, try to keep your movements tight and concentrated. Develop a rhythm and refine your style.

■ Foot Catch and Foot Kick

These add a nice closing flourish to end a simple routine. They come in handy for reversing rope direction, too.

Stand with your right leg slightly in front of your left leg. Begin with a single turn overhead. As the rope approaches your right foot, raise your toes just high enough for the rope to catch under your heel. Don't step on the rope, but hold it taut so that it remains against the bottom of your shoe.

To begin a reverse turn, relax your pull so that the rope can easily slide from under your foot. Remain in position with your left leg behind your right leg and turn the rope

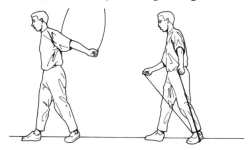

overhead. Anticipate the approach of the rope by raising your left heel. Again, avoid stepping on the rope, but hold it taut against the bottom of your shoe. Relax your pull on the rope to turn it forward again.

The Foot Kick provides a fancy way to get the rope moving again after you catch it with your right foot.

Keeping the rope taut, flatten your right foot and pull it upwards with the rope by raising your arms. Your right leg should bend in about a forty-five-degree angle, and your right heel should barely touch your left knee. Kick your right leg outward, practically straightening it. The rope will sail overhead.

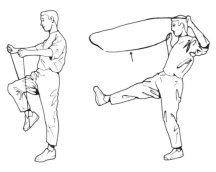

You can use both the Foot Catch and Foot Kick to close your routines, to provide a little visual variety in the middle of a routine, or as a transition between routines.

CHAPTER 3
Dynamic Duos

••••••••••••••••••••••••••••

SHARING YOUR SPACE

When you jump with a partner, you can share a rope, or you can combine two ropes into one routine. Jumping with someone else means learning to synchronize your movements with your partner's movements. Even small movements must be clear, precise, and easy to recognize. You must also turn the rope slowly and steadily, keeping an even rhythm.

Use a slightly longer rope than the one you use for solo jumping. Whether you decide to share a rope or to combine ropes, you and your partner need to start by jumping together with one jumper doing the counting. Try to jump at exactly the same time and to get a feel for one another's rhythm, speed, and style.

■ Getting Ready

Jumpers sharing a rope have very little room to move around. It's a good idea to practice your routines by drawing a three-foot (1m) square box, in which you stand with your partner. Start with both of you facing the same direction. The Jumping Jack works well as a beginning exercise. So do the Heel and Toe Taps. The person turning the rope does the counting.

When the two of you have synchronized your movements, reposition yourselves so that the partner faces the turner. Start again, the turner jumping forward and the partner jumping backwards. Practice the routines in this position.

Next, jump back-to-back.

Finally, stand side-by-side (you'll have to step out of the box for this one), the partner slightly in front of the turner so that the turner's right leg slightly overlaps the partner's left leg. Standing side-by-side might cause you to shrink your movements a bit, but make them as clear and crisp as you can.

With a little practice, you'll be able to link different routines together. For example, you can go from a forward-facing position to a side-by-side position by passing a rope handle from the turner to the partner. In the usual arrangement, the turner stays in one position while the partner changes position.

Some routines, such as the Scissors Step, need to be adjusted when you and your partner jump face-to-face or back-to-back. Instead of moving the same foot forward in a mirror image of each other, use opposite feet to avoid colliding. This also holds true when doing this routine in the side-by-side position. Keep an eye out for routines where such adjustments are necessary. Besides, when moving between positions, changing your footwork adds interest and variety.

In general, the faster you turn the rope, the narrower the space you and your partner will have to jump. A rapidly turning rope peaks more as it revolves and drags less of itself across the ground.

The following lists suggest, in order of difficulty, routines for two jumpers sharing a single rope.

Easy Routines

Basic Jump and
   Balancing Bounce
Jumping Jacks
Running in Place
Side Step
Tiny Kicks

Moderate Routines

Around the World   Scissors Step
Charlie Chaplin   Skier
Half Round   Toe Tap
Heel Tap   Touch Jumps
High Stepping   Twister
Keep On Truckin'

Advanced Routines

Can-Can
Heel Click
Jumping-Jack/Scissors-Step Combination
Right and Left Crisscross

■ Partner Basics

Siamese Twins is a class of routines consisting of two jumpers sharing one rope. Fancy Dancing refers to the technique of meshed turning, in which each jumper has a rope.

Fancy Dancing may seem tricky at first, because jumpers alternate turns and jumps to avoid collisions. You can practice by standing ten feet apart, facing each other, and turning together.

When you become comfortable jumping at the same time, let one person stop, and the other continue. The resting person watches the jumper until ready to rejoin the jump. But this time, the second jumper waits until the first has just cleared the rope before swinging the rope overhead and beginning to jump again. This results in staggered jumping—one jumper's rope passing overhead as the other jumper's rope passes beneath.

The next step involves coming close enough together so that the ropes actually mesh, barely clearing each other. This means you must become extra sensitive to the rhythm of your partner's turning.

Siamese Twins and Fancy Dancing routines come in all shapes and sizes. The next section teaches you some of the more interesting ones.

SIAMESE TWINS

As the name suggests, when two jumpers share the same rope they should appear as one jumper. You and your partner also need to agree beforehand just how many counts to take before one of you changes position. Neither jumper wants to be surprised in the middle of a routine.

Remember to draw the three-foot (1m) square box to keep your jumping tight and focused. As you become more accustomed to sharing your space, you'll need the box less and less.

■ Spoons

Jumper 1 holds the rope, stepping in front of it. Jumper 2 stands with her back to Jumper 1, as in the illustration. On the count of three, Jumper 1 swings the rope overhead, and both jumpers take the first jump with feet together, keeping their arms close to their sides. As the rope swings overhead, both jumpers take a balancing bounce and prepare for the next jump, feet together. After ten jumps, they stop.

■ Visiting

Jumper 1 stands in the box alone, as Jumper 2 stands to the side a few feet away. On the count of three, Jumper 1 takes the first jump feet together, and a balancing bounce as the rope passes overhead. Jumper 1 counts out loud while jumping.

Jumper 2 does not share the rope at this point, but closely watches Jumper 1 and jumps along in place. At the count of 15, just as Jumper 1 clears the rope, Jumper 2 rushes inside the rope and takes the spoons position in front of Jumper 1. Now both partners jump together until the count of 20, when Jumper 2 exits the rope.

■ Visit and Switch

Nicely done, this routine makes a very impressive show. Practice Visiting, turning the rope faster and faster, until both jumpers gain confidence.

Jumper 1 stands in the box alone. Jumper 2 stands to the side. On the count of three, Jumper 1 takes the first jump feet together, plus a balancing bounce as the rope passes overhead. On the count of 15, Jumper 2 rushes inside and takes the Spoons position in front of Jumper 1. Remember, both jumpers should keeps their arms close to their sides.

At some agreed-upon count, say 25, just as the rope approaches its zenith, Jumper 1 quickly passes the right handle of the rope to Jumper 2. For the next jump, each jumper holds a separate handle. Continue jumping this way for another five counts, at which point Jumper 1 passes the left handle of the rope to Jumper 2. Now Jumper 1, the original turner, may exit the rope sideways at any time, leaving Jumper 2 to turn alone.

■ Kissin' Cousins

You and your partner might want to practice for this routine by first doing a few solo reverse or back jumps. Remember, jumping backwards means anticipating, rather than actually seeing, the rope as it approaches your heels. You do this by carefully listening to the rhythm of the rope as you turn it.

Jumper 1 holds the rope, stepping in front of it. Jumper 2 stands very close, facing Jumper 1. On the count of three, Jumper 1 turns the rope overhead. Both partners take the first jump feet together, with Jumper 2 jumping backwards over the rope. Jumpers take a balancing bounce between jumps and continue jumping to the count of ten.

Now switch places so that the forward jumper becomes the reverse jumper. Practice the routine until both you and your partner become comfortable with jumping backwards. Gradually increase your speed while staying together.

■ Visiting Cousins

This is the simple Visiting routine adapted to face-to-face jumping. On the count of three, Jumper 1 takes the first jump feet together, while Jumper 2 stands to the side a few feet away. On the count of 15, just as Jumper 1 clears the rope, Jumper 2 rushes inside the rope and takes the Kissin' Cousins position (page 47). Both partners jump together this way to the count of 20, when Jumper 2 exits the rope.

■ Switching Cousins

A bit trickier than the original Visit and Switch, Switching Cousins not only requires that the rope handles pass from Jumper 1 to Jumper 2, who stand face-to-face, but that both jumpers get used to turning the rope in opposite directions during the switch. For example, after Jumper 2 enters the rope and the count reaches 25, Jumper 1 passes the right rope handle to Jumper 2's left hand. Now Jumper 2 turns the rope backwards with the left hand, while Jumper 1 continues to turn the rope forward with the left hand. After five counts, Jumper 1 passes the left rope handle to Jumper 2's right hand, leaving Jumper 2 turning and jumping backwards. Jumper 1 may exit at this point.

■ Sun and Moon

This is a variation of Around the World (page 31). In this case, the rope turner (Jumper 1) revolves a quarter turn with each jump, while Jumper 2, sharing the rope, remains stationary. This means that although both jump together, Jumper 2 exits the rope without having to move.

Jumper 2 continues to jump in place while Jumper 1 continues rotating in quarter turns. Soon, the rope approaches its original position, and Jumper 2 can rejoin Jumper 1.

■ Side-by-Side and Variations

This straightforward routine begins with the jumpers standing side-by-side, each holding one of the rope handles. They may also link hands if they wish. Jumpers step over the rope and, on the count of three, swing the rope overhead and take the first jump feet together. Try to jump at exactly the same time to the same height. This also holds true for the balancing bounces between jumps.

Since each jumper controls a rope handle, one can easily move behind the other, changing the Side-by-Side position into the Visit and Switch position. At this point, the partners continue jumping together, one may exit, or both may resume the Side-by-Side position.

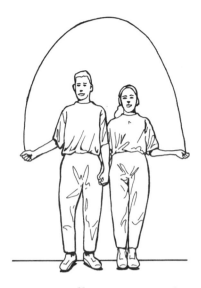

Side-by-side jumping allows you to do some familiar routines in tandem. Remember the Heel Tap? Do it with your partner, tapping either the same or opposite heels. You can stagger the routine so that one partner jumps as the other one does the Heel Tap. In fact, with the exception of the Side Step, all of the Fancy Footwork routines work in a Side-by-Side step. Running in Place works particularly well.

If you change from Side-by-Side to Visit and Switch, remember to concentrate on routines that do not take up too much of your partner's space. Two people standing close together should not even think about doing a routine like Can-Can!

You can also vary the Side-by-Side position by standing alongside your partner, facing the opposite direction. This means that as the rope turns, one person jumps forward while the other jumps backwards. This skill will come in handy when you learn Chinese Wheel (page 53).

If jumping Siamese Twins–style makes you claustrophobic, the next section allows more room for both style and creativity.

FANCY DANCING

In Fancy Dancing, two ropes and two jumpers combine into one routine. This means you and your partner need to master the technique of staggered turning so that one rope hits the ground as the other rope reaches its zenith, and one person jumps while the other person takes a balancing bounce.

If you and your partner easily turn and count together, thinking in half time may help you learn staggered jumping. Jumper 1 begins to jump, counting "one *and*, two *and*, three *and* . . ." with the *number* indicating the actual jump, while the "*and*" indicates the bounce. Jumper 2 remains in place and counts along with Jumper 1. However, Jumper 2 starts his *number* count at Jumper 1's "*and*." Both jumpers should continue counting this way until they feel comfortable.

Now Jumper 2 starts jumping along with Jumper 1. But Jumper 2 takes the first jump just as the rope passes over the head of Jumper 1. Similarly, Jumper 1 clears the rope just as it passes over the head of Jumper 2. Jumping and bouncing occur at the same time, producing a unifying element.

Practice staggered jumping at various speeds while standing side-by-side.

■ Forward Eggbeater

When you and your partner can do staggered jumping like clockwork, you are ready to try meshing ropes in this routine.

Stand facing one another at a distance of about ten feet (3m). Jumper 1 starts jumping and Jumper 2 joins in. When you both have a good, steady rhythm, Jumper 2 moves a little closer to Jumper 1 with each jump, until the two ropes practically touch. Each rope actually rotates for an instant in the other rope's space and must clear out in

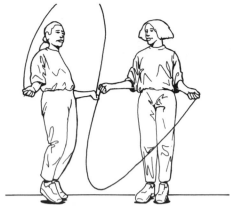

time to avoid a collision. The action may remind you of an eggbeater.

After a few minutes of this, you or your partner moves backwards until the ropes are totally clear of each other.

■ Reverse Eggbeater

This is the Eggbeater with both jumpers turning their ropes backwards. You'll find it challenging to jump forward towards your partner while turning the rope backwards.

■ Back-to-Back Eggbeater

This routine consists of the Forward Eggbeater with the jumpers starting out facing away from each other. Of

course, Jumper 2 must remain keenly aware of Jumper 1's rhythm, since the rope can't be seen. When you master this one, try reversing the direction of the rope.

■ Chinese Wheel

Jumper 2 stands next to Jumper 1, but facing the opposite direction. With the left hand, Jumper 1 takes the right handle of Jumper 2's rope. With the right hand, Jumper 2 takes the left handle of Jumper 1's rope. This means the jumpers are turning not only their own rope, but their partner's rope as well.

To accomplish staggered jumping in this position, each jumper must also stagger the turning motion between hands. With a little practice, you won't find this difficult at all.

Now the partners jump together, each doing a jumping jack while the other actually jumps. You can try this with other routines as well. Both the Scissors Step and Tiny Kicks work well.

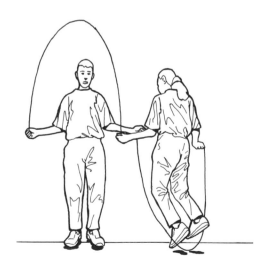

CHAPTER 4
"No Hands" Jumping

....

JUMPING IN GROUPS

"No Hands" Jumping means that two people turn the rope, leaving the jumper or jumpers free to do longer and more elaborate routines. But it can also mean that a jumper gives up control over the speed or height of the rope. This has led to two styles of jumping: Group Jumping and Double Dutch.

In Group Jumping, the turners may cooperate with the jumpers—or not—and the number of jumpers is limited only by the length of the rope. One of the jumpers may be named the leader and get to direct the others. In Double Dutch, jumpers and turners make up a team, and usually no more than two people jump at a time.

■ Learning the Ropes

For both Group and Double Dutch Jumping, you'll want a rope at least 12 feet (3.6m) long and properly weighted so that it cuts through the air easily. You can make such a rope by purchasing a 24-foot (7m) long piece of cotton sash cord from a hardware store, doubling it over, and twisting the halves together. Tape the rope at the middle, then finish the rope by tying a double knot at each end.

To hold the rope securely, grip the end of the rope in your fist so that the knot sticks out near your little finger. You can also hold the knot in the palm of your hand, but slide your index finger between the two strands of the the rope to keep it from slipping. Turn the rope by making wide circles with your arm, from the shoulder.

■ Entering the Rope

There are no hard and fast rules for entering the rope in a Group Jumping situation. Usually, the turners begin revolving the rope at a moderate speed while the jumpers wait side by side, holding hands. At a signal from the leader of the group, all rush in and begin jumping. Now the turners may do as they wish, but they probably want the jumpers to succeed—at least for a little while!

Jumping in a group is challenging and fun. Many of the solo routines you learned earlier adapt well to group jumping. But here are a few new ones, specially designed for groups of four or more.

■ Jumping in a Row

This is the simplest of all Group Jumping routines. Jumpers stand side by side, link hands, and wait outside the rope. The leader of the group stands at one end of the line and gives directions.

When the leader gives the signal, all rush in and begin jumping at once, stretched along the length of the rope. The jumpers take a balancing bounce between each jump.

In one variation, the leader shouts "Front" and takes a step or two forward. Now the line pivots from the center jumper, so that the leader jumps slightly ahead of the second jumper, who jumps slightly ahead of the third jumper, and so on. When the leader shouts "Line," the jumpers return to their original positions. When the leader shouts "Back" and takes a step or two backward, the line pivots in the opposite direction, so that the last jumper is the first to meet the rope, followed by the next-to-last jumper, and so on.

A/C   **Line**

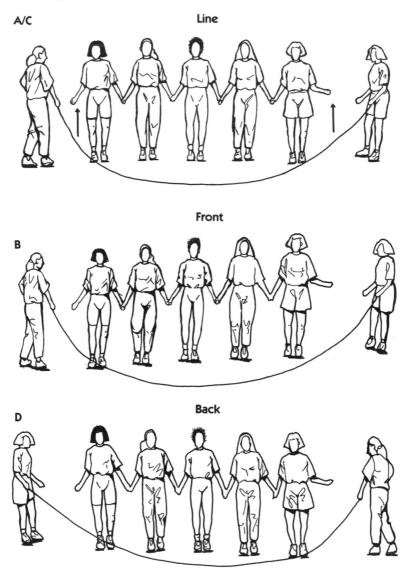

Front

Back

■ Traveller

Although this routine involves more than two jumpers, the basic technique will remind you of the Spoons jump (page 45). You'll need a slightly longer rope, however.

An even number of people stand side by side in a line. The traveller stands behind the line.

The traveller begins jumping directly behind the first person in the line. Suddenly she swings the rope over him so that he must jump along in a Spoons formation. This can last for an agreed-upon number of jumps or as long as you want. Both jumpers can improvise. Eventually, the traveller releases the first person in line and moves on to the second, who now jumps along. Then the traveller moves on to the third, and so on.

Let's say you have four people in line. After the traveller releases the fourth one, she jumps back to resume

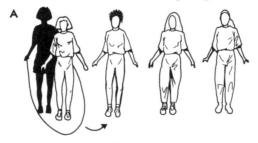

her position behind the first person. But now the other jumpers double up. The traveller swings the rope over a pair of jumpers, who must jump in unison. Then she releases them and moves to the second pair of jumpers.

The final step takes some practice, but makes an impressive show. The two pairs of jumpers come together to make a group of four. The traveller, letting out her rope a little, swings it over the entire group, which jumps in unison with her.

■ Rainbow

For this routine you need five people and three ropes. Everyone stands in a line. The two outside turners have the longest rope. Within that rope stand two turners with a rope of their own and, between them, a single jumper with his own rope.

At a signal from the lead turner, everyone begins turning in unison. The two outside people only turn the rope, while the two inside people jump as well as turn. In the center, the single jumper also jumps and turns.

When this routine is performed cleanly, you can easily see why it's called Rainbow!

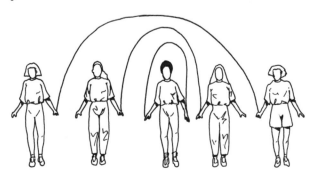

■ Organ Pipes

Jumpers stand on one side of the rope holding hands. At a count of three, they rush into the rope and, still holding hands, begin jumping together, taking a balancing bounce between each jump.

First 3–4 jumps

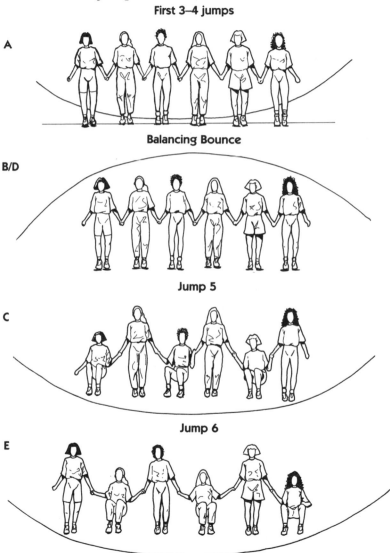

Balancing Bounce

Jump 5

Jump 6

After three or four jumps, every other jumper crouches for the next jump, then stands erect for the following jump while his neighbor crouches. This means that for every turn of the rope, the jumpers are alternating crouching with standing.

All the jumpers stand erect for the balancing bounce. This means that jumpers have to get into or out of a crouching position during that short interval when the rope passes overhead and begins to descend.

■ Two Loops

You'll need a very long rope for this routine—at least 40 feet (12 m) long. Starting with her hand near her waist, the first turner makes a wide circle with her end of the rope. When her hand is at the highest point, the second turner begins her circle. This makes it look as if the long rope is breaking into two sections—almost as if an invisible turner is standing at the center. Two or more jumpers enter these sections and may run around to switch sides.

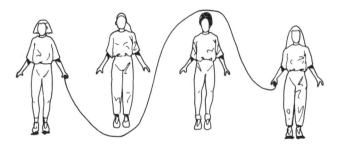

■ Umbrella

You can perform this routine with as few as four turners and as many as ten, but you always need an even number. You will only need half as many long ropes as jumpers.

All the turners stand in a wide circle, each turner facing his partner. At a signal from the lead turner, everyone starts turning at once, so that all the ropes rise and fall together, sort of like a trampoline or an umbrella.

One jumper may enter the ropes and jump through the sections of the umbrella, or several jumpers may chase each other through the sections. If you have many jumpers, you can have a moving circle, or a circle within a circle. The possibilities are many!

DOUBLE DUTCH BASICS

Jumping Double Dutch, a familiar activity on city streets a generation ago, is enjoying a huge comeback. "Double" refers to the basic setup: two ropes, two turners, and two or more jumpers. The turners rotate the ropes at the same time but in opposite directions, "egg-beater" style—both ropes turning inward.

The jumpers run into the turning ropes and do anything from simple jumping to elaborate and even acrobatic routines. Jumpers and turners make up a single team, and Double Dutch jumping is considered a team sport. This means that the jumpers and turners cooperate and work things out ahead of time, like how fast the rope will turn and for how long.

■ Doubles and Singles Teams

While the usual set of jumpers—called a doubles team—consists of four people, two turning and two jumping, a solo jumper may enter the ropes, and perform a number of routines. This is a great way for one jumper to show off acrobatics. The "egg-beater" style of turning remains the same. One jumper and two turners make up a singles team. Either a singles or a doubles team may enter an officially sponsored competition.

But whether you belong to a singles or doubles team, you'll find that friendly teamwork delivers the best results. Be open-minded and flexible when you're putting together your team. Allow every member to have a turn at jumping.

■ Turning and Jumping

Make two long ropes out of cotton sash cord. For a singles team, each rope should measure 12 feet (3.5m) long. For a doubles team, the ropes should measure no more than 14 feet (4m) long.

If you want two 12-foot (3.5m) ropes for your singles team, buy 48 feet (14.5m) of sash cord. If you want two 14-foot (4m) ropes for your doubles team, buy 56 feet (17m) of sash cord. Cut the piece into four equal sections. Twist two sections together for each rope, taping them at the middle and double knotting the ends.

Turners hold the ends of the ropes as they would for Group Jumping. Both turners need to stand with their backs straight and feet slightly apart. Good posture helps create a solid, wobble-free turn. Before starting, the turners drop their arms in a relaxed position so that the ropes lie beside each other on the ground.

One turner starts turning by first rocking one of the ropes back and forth while counting. On the third count, the turners swing that rope inward, and then follow it with the second rope, also swinging it inward. Both turners move their arms in wide circles from the shoulder, striving for an even, rhythmic motion.

If part of a singles team, the jumper enters the ropes from either side or either end, from slightly behind the turner's shoulder. Jumpers on a doubles team enter the same way. They may also enter one behind the other, or at the same time from opposite ends, or from behind the left and right shoulders of a turner.

The most important concern for a jumper or pair of jumpers is to clear the ropes. Once inside, jumpers move to the center of the ropes where the arch is highest. The basic jump consists of hopping from one foot to the other with no balancing bounces in between. Jumpers may keep their arms straight at their sides, place their hands on hips, or bend their arms at the elbows as if jogging. The arms should not stick out or wave away from the body.

A jumper always exits the ropes by facing towards one of the turners, and then running out at about a 45-degree angle. Never attempt to chase the rope by running directly behind it. Jumpers should bend only slightly to avoid colliding with the ropes, but not so much as to obstruct their view of what's ahead.

ROUTINES, PLAIN AND FANCY

It's important to understand that the term "Double Dutch" refers to nothing more than the setup of ropes, turners, and jumpers. The beauty and fun of Double Dutch jumping lies in the freedom you have to invent acrobatic or dancelike routines. Start by just practicing and enjoying jumping with your team. You can begin with the following basic routines for a single jumper or a pair of synchronized jumpers.

■ Simple Hip-Hop

Turners rotate the ropes slowly as the jumper enters from either side. Once inside, the jumper takes the first two jumps with both feet together, hops with the right foot for the third turn and with the left foot for the fourth turn. During this hopping from foot to foot, the turners gradually increase the speed of the ropes. To avoid tripping, the jumper needs to make sure to lift the resting foot as high as possible.

Turners want to test the jumpers' speed, not trip them. The jumpers should call out when they feel they can't go any faster. From that moment on, the turners need to slow down the ropes, allowing the jumper to exit.

■ High Tide

Turn the ropes at a moderate speed. The jumper enters from either side and begins to hop, alternating feet. When feeling comfortable the jumper calls out, "High tide." Gradually, the turners raise the ropes so that the jumper has to hop higher and higher to clear them. When this becomes too difficult, the jumper calls out, "Low tide," and the turners drop the ropes to ground level again.

■ The Irish Jig

This is a basic Heel Tap without balancing bounces. Turners spin the ropes at a slow to moderate speed. The jumper enters the ropes, takes the first two jumps with both feet together, then hops on alternate feet, doing a Heel Tap each time for the following jumps. To add a little style, the jumper can rest, hands on hips, and put a little extra spring into the hops.

■ Running in Circles

Turn the ropes slowly for this one. After entering, the

jumper runs in place, lifting each foot high enough to clear the ropes, holding slightly bent arms to the sides as if jogging. After remaining stationary for about ten jumps, the jumper begins turning in a clockwise direction, blind for a moment to the approach of one of the ropes. After making a full revolution, the jumper runs in place for a little while and then exits.

Many of the "Fancy Footwork" and "Getting Physical" routines are also good for Double Dutch jumping. However, it's important to master a routine thoroughly before trying it in Double Dutch. Jumping over two ropes, turning in opposite directions, requires a bit of concentration at first! As your confidence grows, you'll begin to appreciate the fact that you no longer have to turn the ropes. Your arms and hands can move along with your routine, and this can be very effective.

Moving on from the basics, here are two more elaborate routines for doubles and larger groups of jumpers.

■ Jumping Beans

The jumpers stand at opposite sides of the rope. The first jumper runs in, hops twice, then runs out the other side. As the first jumper exits, the second jumper runs in, hops twice, and runs out the opposite side. Each jumper continues to enter and hop twice as the previous one exits.

Each jumper may also challenge the other jumpers to imitate him by adding some new movement each time. The rope turners may also surprise the jumpers by varying the speed of the ropes.

■ Double Dutch Within Double Dutch

As the name suggests, this routine involves a pair of turners spinning their ropes in Double Dutch formation. A second pair of turners, also spinning Double Dutch, jump inside the first pair's rope. If you like, you can add a single jumper or two jumpers in the middle. It looks great.

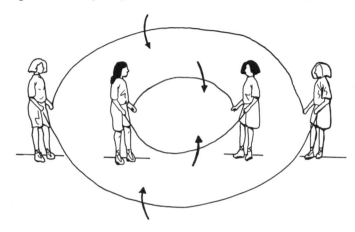

DOUBLE DUTCH RHYMES

Music adds sparkle to any Double Dutch routine, but if finding the right kind of music or equipment on which to play it requires too much effort, you can substitute a rhyme.

You already know a few rhymes from the first chapter. Double Dutch rhymes add to the fun with nonsense verses. They can also provide singsong instructions, inviting jumpers to join in.

Here's a great rhyme for three or more jumpers. The first jumper begins the rhyme while the others wait outside the rope:

My mother, your mother—yap, yap, yap!
They chatter on the telephone and never seem to
    stop.

They stay at home all day, and they hardly ever
   visit.
When someone rings the doorbell, it's me who yells,
   "Who is it?"

At this point, one of the waiting jumpers shouts his or her name and joins the first jumper. Now the two jumpers recite:

My father, your father—yuck, yuck, yuck!
They play poker every night and complain about
   their luck.
They watch TV on Saturdays to see their favorites
   win.
When someone knocks the knocker, it's me who
   yells, "Come in!"

Now the last waiting jumper joins in. All three jumpers recite this final part:

My brothers, your sisters—tsk, tsk tsk!
They'll never lift a finger to wash a dirty dish.
They sleep all afternoon, and they're getting pretty
   stout.
When someone steals the silverware, it's me who
   yells, "Get out!"

The first and second jumpers exit the rope, leaving the third jumper to begin the verse from the top. Each jumper may change the verse to make it funnier, or to suit the individual players.

Here's another rhyme that challenges the jumper to pantomime the motions suggested in the verse:

Three unlucky circus clowns snuck into the town
To knock the king upon the head and steal his
   golden crown.

Bobby Banana waved a white-and-blue bandanna,
Alfred Potato was juggling three tomatoes,
But Crazy Colonel Jess was really quite a mess
And forgot to wear his shoes,
So he tippy-toed back home and bought the *Daily
News.*
All night he looked it over but didn't know what it
said,
So he turned off the light and crawled into bed.

And another rhyme, not for the bashful:

Down in the meadow where the green grass grows,
Sat little (name of first jumper), sniffin' at a rose.
She sang so high and she sang so sweet,
That along came (name of second jumper) and
kissed her on the cheek.
He kissed her on the cheek, and he kissed her once
again.
She wanted him to stop, but she couldn't say just
when.
So along came (name of third jumper), a big,
strong lout,
And without a single word, he pushed (name of
second jumper) out!

You can also invent your own rhymes, tailoring them to
fit the personalities of your teammates or to advertise the
qualities of your team.

In the next section, you'll learn how to get serious about
Double Dutch.

JUMP ROPE ORGANIZATIONS

In recent years, many organizations have been set up to promote rope skipping on a regional, national, and even international level. Most of them share the dream of making rope skipping an Olympic sport. The dream may soon come true, thanks to the efforts of the following:

■ United States Rope Skipping Association (USRSA)

In January of 1995, the International Rope Skipping Organization (IRSO) and the World Rope Skipping Federation (WRSF) merged, creating the United States Rope Skipping Association. You can contact its president, Roger Crozier, at Post Office Box 8160, Richmond, Indiana 47374, telephone/FAX (317) 966-9773.

The USRSA will function as an umbrella organization for teams all over the United States. It will continue the activities of the IRSO and WRSF on a much larger scale. These activities include workshops and tournaments, regional and national competitions, and jump rope camps for children and adults.

Its European counterpart, the European Rope Skipping Organization (ERSO) will sponsor teams all over Western and Eastern Europe, the United Kingdom, Australia, and Canada.

You can join the USRSA by contacting it directly or through one of its many teams or affiliated organizations. A few are listed below. Your membership fee entitles you to a quarterly newsletter.

USRSA Teams
Coronado Speed Spinners
600 Sixth Street
Coronado, California 92118
Coach: Amy Steward

Indy Air Bears
5814 South Arlington Avenue
Indianapolis, Indiana 46237
Coach: Niki Glover

Lincoln Lions
22 Tallyho Road
Cumberland, Rhode Island 02864
Coach: Byron Kinniburgh

Blue & White Rope Skippers
17 Limes Avenue
Stratford-on-Avon, Warwickshire
CV37 9BQ, United Kingdom
Coach: Roger Smithies

Lethbridge Bombers
421 Normandy Road South
Lethbridge, Alberta, Canada T1J 3X9
Coach: Cliff Bogdan

The Australian Rope Skipping Organization or T.E.A.M.
Post Office Box 210
Riverstone 2765, NSW, Australia
Contact: Greg Bannerman

■ **Canadian Skipping Organization (CSA)**

This organization functions much like the USRSA, sponsoring teams throughout the Canadian provinces. It also holds annual regional and national competitions, as well as organizing camps for children and adults. You can contact the CSA through its secretary, Christine Willoughby, 5511 44 St., Drayton Valley, Alberta, Canada T7A 1B4, telephone (403) 542–4406; FAX (403) 542–7617.

■ Jump Rope for Heart

The National Heart Foundation of Australia, in association with the Australian Council for Health, Physical Education and Recreation (ACHPER), has created this wonderful program for schools. Jump Rope for Heart has operated in over 90 percent of Australian schools since 1983. More than five million children take part. Participating schools receive a free resource kit, including ropes and teaching materials. At the end of the program, a fund-raising "Jump Off" marathon is held, and ten percent of the funds raised are returned to the school in the form of a rebate.

Some state divisions of the Heart Foundation run skipping competitions and tournaments, but the main focus of Jump Rope for Heart is on demonstrations. Currently there are over 100 demonstration teams that perform 1,000 demonstrations per year to live audiences of over two million people. To contact this organization, you can write to:

Jump Rope for Heart
National Heart Foundation of Australia
Post Office Box 2
WODEN ACT 2606, Australia
Attn: Cameron Prout, National Coordinator

■ American Double Dutch League (ADDL)

Founded in 1975 by former police detectives Ulysses Williams and David Walker, the ADDL traces its roots back to the previous year, when both men began organizing Harlem schoolchildren into Double Dutch teams that would compete against each other in annual competitions.

The ADDL continues to sponsor annual regional and national tournaments for boys and girls in the fifth through twelfth grades. The rules of their competitions have become a standard for many other rope skipping organizations.

You can contact the ADDL at the following address:

American Double Dutch League
132 West 109th Street
New York, NY 10025

■ Entering an ADDL-Sponsored Competition

Both boys and girls may enter an ADDL competition. To qualify, you must be in the fifth through twelfth grade. For grades below high school, all members of singles and doubles teams must be the same age. At the high school level, team members do not have to be the same age, but all must be ninth through twelfth graders.

As mentioned before, you can form either a singles team with two turners and one jumper, or a doubles team with two turners and two jumpers. Line up a substitute player in case of emergencies, but make sure to register the substitute's name with the judges at the beginning of the competition. A substitute may come in before, but not during, one of the three official ADDL tests.

■ What to Expect

Your team will undergo three tests. The first measures jumping speed, the second measures accuracy in the execution of compulsory routines, and the third looks for imagination in freestyle routines. This last test gives you the chance to pull out all the stops and really show your stuff.

■ Preparing to Compete

Teamwork is the key. Avoid having one person or just a pair of people doing *all the jumping* for all three tests.

ADDL rules don't require jumpers and turners to switch places for each test, but it certainly gives the impression that you belong to a well-rounded team if they do. In other words, a professional impression counts, and your team's versatility will look good to the judges, especially when you are competing against faster, flashier, but one-jumper teams.

Also, if your turners are going to jump, keep in mind that jumpers and turners may only trade places at the beginning of each test.

■ 1—The Speed Test

For this test, judges want to see how many times the jumper or pair of jumpers can jump in two minutes. The turners begin rotating the ropes very fast while the jumper waits at either side or either end of the rope. If there are two jumpers, they wait at opposite ends behind the left and right shoulders of the turners.

At a signal from one of the turners, the jumper or jumpers rush in, and the judges start the stopwatch. Judges expect to see a clean hop from foot to foot as the ropes pass beneath the jumpers. A pair of jumpers must be perfectly synchronized.

At the end of two minutes, a buzzer goes off, and the results are recorded. Well-conditioned jumpers should be able to do about 300 jumps in this time span, but again the jumps must look clean and well executed. Poorly performed jumps may be subtracted from the total count.

■ 2—The Compulsory Routines Test

For this test, jumpers must perform five compulsory routines with speed, grace, and good jumping form.

The first routine requires the jumper to turn clockwise in two full circles while hopping on the right foot. For the second routine, the jumper must revolve counterclockwise by hopping on the left foot.

The third routine requires two right-foot crisscross jumps (the right foot in front of the left foot).

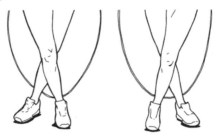

The fourth routine consists of two left-foot crisscross jumps.

Finally, the fifth routine demands ten high steps—alternating jumps in which you lift your knee up to your chest.

The jumper of a singles team has only 30 seconds to do all five routines in order. The jumpers of a doubles team have 40 seconds to do all the routines, but they must be done in unison.

■ 3—The Freestyle Routines Test

This is where your team can really shine. Singles and doubles teams have one minute to do between three and five routines. Anything goes in the way of acrobatics, but props such as balls or batons may be used only in one of the tricks.

Recently, judges have relaxed the rules to allow more than two jumpers to participate in the freestyle test. Statewide champions now compete at the national level with stunning displays of acrobatic feats.

CHAPTER 5
Fun and Fancy

●●●●●●●●●●●●●●●●●●●●●●●●●●●●

TWIRLING TRICKS

You don't always have to jump over the rope to have fun with it. The following routines demonstrate how various twirling skills can not only entertain you, but help improve your agility and coordination—both important for a solid, polished jumping technique.

■ Waist Wrap

This routine helps sharpen the reverse turn. Hold both handles of the rope in your right hand (or left hand, if that's what you prefer). Gently twirl the rope overhead like a helicopter, in a counterclockwise direction. Keep it moving just fast enough to stay high. As the rope travels forward around your right side, bring your right hand down to waist level and raise your left hand overhead. Allow the rope to wrap around your waist.

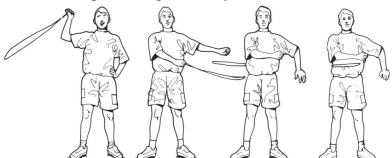

When the rope unwraps itself, raise your right hand and lower your left hand. Twirl the rope overhead in a clockwise direction now. As the rope travels back around your right side, bring your right hand down again and raise your left hand. Allow the rope to wrap around your waist in the opposite direction.

A variation of this routine consists of switching hands during the brief moment the rope completes its wrap before beginning to unwrap.

■ Open Waist Wrap

This variation introduces a closed and an open rope to the basic Waist Wrap.

Take a handle of the rope in each hand. Keeping your hands together, twirl the rope overhead in a counterclockwise direction. As the rope circles to the front, bring your left hand down behind your back and continue to circle your right hand overhead. As the rope comes around again, bring your right hand down to waist level.

Unwrapping the rope involves lifting your right hand overhead and reversing direction.

■ Shoulder Wrap

With both rope handles in your right hand, hold your right arm slightly out to the side and bent at the elbow. Twirl the rope forward just fast enough to keep it taut.

As the rope begins to come down, jut out your right elbow and pull your hand up to your right armpit. The rope wraps around your right shoulder.

Give the rope a little flick with your left hand to assist

it in unwrapping; then twirl the rope backwards with the right hand. After a few swings, as the rope begins to pass back overhead, quickly pass the rope handles from your right hand to your left hand. Continue swinging the rope backwards with your left hand, your left arm slightly out and bent at the elbow.

As the rope passes back overhead again, jut out your left elbow and pull your hand up to your left armpit. The rope wraps around your left shoulder.

After you've helped it unwrap again, repeat the routine.

■ Figure Eights

Learning to pass the rope smoothly between hands will give you confidence in routines such as Visiting Cousins, where you must pass the rope to a partner. The skill also comes in handy as a transitional movement when you begin to combine routines into longer sequences.

Hold both handles of the rope in one hand. Twirl the rope at your side in a clockwise direction. Avoid spinning it too fast. When the rope points straight out in front of you, pass the handles to the opposite hand and continue twirling. Make the motion smooth and seamless so that the rope never falters as it moves. When you've mastered clockwise twirling, reverse direction.

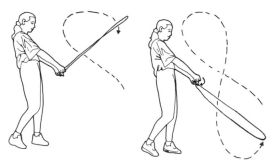

As you pass the rope handles from one hand to another, you'll find the rope tracing a figure eight in the air.

■ Leg Over Eights

Having practiced the previous routine really pays off when learning this one. Twirl the rope at your right side in a clockwise direction. As the rope points straight out in front of you, and you prepare to switch hands, raise your left leg high enough so that you can pass the rope under it. Make the motion smooth and seamless.

Work on twirling the rope a set number of times before you pass it under your leg to the opposite hand. When you've mastered this motion, do no more than two twirls on each side before passing the rope.

Now reverse the direction. As you prepare to pass the rope from your right hand to your left, notice that you must now raise your right leg. Practice this until you can do only two twirls on each side before passing the rope.

▪ Samurai Warrior

With your right hand at shoulder level, twirl the rope counterclockwise in front of you. As the rope approaches its highest point, bring your hand behind your head so that the rope makes one turn in back of you. As the rope ascends again, move your right hand in front to its original position. After one turn, move your hand back as before, and so on. Placing your left hand on your waist will help to stabilize you.

▪ Bolas

With this technique, you hold the rope in the middle. Stretch a two-foot (60cm) section of the rope between your hands and, holding it in the middle, twirl the ends of the rope in opposite directions. You can make either large or small circles, depending on how much of the rope you stretch between your hands.

Bolas is fun to do and impressive to watch, but be careful when attempting it. The fast-moving rope handles can accidentally strike you.

ROPE GAMES

Most of the following games use a long rope that swings, stretches, or squiggles rather than turns. Some use teams and have rules; others just give you an excuse to show off and get silly. All present physical challenges that will help you improve your overall jumping technique.

■ High Water, Low Water

Players line up to jump over the rope, which two crouching turners stretch (but do not turn) about five inches (12 cm) above the floor. Each player takes a turn jumping over the rope and then runs back around the turners and lines up again. When all the players have jumped, the turners raise the rope another five inches, and the players begin again. The turners continue to raise the rope until only one player remains—the winner.

■ Over the Waves

This game resembles High Water, Low Water except that the turners wiggle the rope up and down to form waves to jump over. When all the players have jumped once, the waves become more and more violent, until only one player, the best "swimmer," remains.

▪ Rock the Cradle

Rock the Cradle is a two-team game. The turners stand, swinging the rope back and forth like a rocking cradle. Players of each team line up on opposite sides of the rope. At the signal, teams alternate sending players into the rope. Each player must jump over the swinging rope three times before running through to the other side. A player who trips is out of the game.

When all the players have jumped, the turners raise the rope. The remaining player wins the round for his team; the team winning two out of three rounds takes the game.

▪ Squiggling Snake

The two turners crouch while holding the rope, wiggling it from side to side so that it resembles a snake. The first player jumps over the rope at one end near a turner. Then he must straddle the rope, hopping from foot to foot along the entire rope length, towards the opposite turner. The player must take wide hops to avoid brushing the squiggling snake. The first player to hop from turner to turner wins.

▪ Running the Gauntlet

This game consists of two teams, each with six members. One player from each team takes a handle of the rope. The remaining players line up on opposite sides of the rope.

At a signal, the turners spin the rope in either direction, and the teams alternate sending a player into the rope. Players must run completely through the rope without getting tangled up and without making any jumps. A player who fails to make it through goes out of the game, and the team with one player left wins the first round.

Two new turners take the rope handles, and the teams line up for the second round. The team winning two out of three rounds takes the game.

■ Daisy Chain

A Daisy Chain can have as many as six jumpers, but for starters, limit your chain to three good jumpers. The jumpers stand side-by-side and link hands. At the count of three, the jumpers rush into the turning rope and jump together, keeping their hands linked (A). After a few jumps, the two end jumpers join hands to form a circle. Now all the jumpers revolve in a circle while continuing to jump (B).

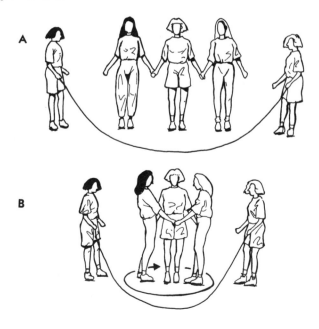

At the end of the routine, the jumpers break the circle, jump in a line again, and exit one by one.

■ Jump and Duck

Attach a soft weight, such as an old shoe, to the end of a rope. The rope should be no more than six feet (2m) long, so you might have to double over a 12-foot (4m) long Double Dutch rope. One player holds the other end of the rope and spins around so that the rope makes a sweeping circular motion. Even though the player in the center is standing, the weighted end of the rope swings close to the ground.

One by one, the remaining players run in and jump over the spinning rope as it whizzes by. The center player may spin faster, bringing the rope higher, or raise it to the point where the jumpers must jump very high to clear it or duck to get under it safely! Of course, a truly devious spinner might dip it down and raise it high during a single revolution, so that the players must make some snap decisions about whether to jump or to duck.

■ Circle of Poison

With chalk, draw a large circle on the ground, no more than four feet (1.2m) in diameter. Find a very long rope, at least 20 feet (6m), or tie two 14-foot (4m) Double

Dutch ropes together to make one long rope. Tie the ends of this rope together securely to make a loop.

Four players get inside the loop, space themselves evenly apart, and pull away from each other, so that the stretched rope makes a kind of square, with each player standing in a corner of the square and the "circle of poison" in the center. Players may not hold on to the rope, but keep the square taut by pressing their backs against it.

At the signal, a tug-of-war begins as each player tries to drag the others into the poison circle. The only time players may handle the rope is if it should slip down from their waist. When a player is dragged into the circle by another player, the "poisoned" player exits the rope, leaving the remaining players to tough it out.

The player who manages to drag the last opponent into the circle wins the game.

WORKING OUT

Besides using your rope for jumping routines and group games, you can easily turn it into a valuable exercise tool. The exercises in this chapter combine effectiveness with fun, and they work for men, women, boys, and girls.

The principle behind these exercises is *isometrics*. In isometric exercises, the muscles exert force against each other, rather than against a dead weight. The effect is the same as when you do sit-ups, push-ups, or pull-ups.

Isometric exercises also require very little time. The average exercise lasts between eight and ten seconds, so you can do an entire set, even with rest breaks, in just a few minutes.

To transform an ordinary jump rope into an exercise tool, tie the ends together in an adjustable slipknot.

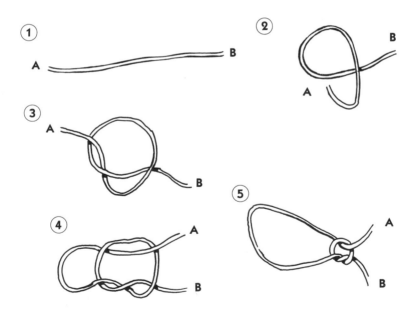

The handle of the rope keeps the knot from slipping off, but allow the knot to slip inward, shortening the loop. For even shorter loops, you can fold the rope over itself.

It's a good idea to take a few precautions when using a rope for isometric exercises. If possible, wear gloves to avoid the possibility of rope burns. For those exercises where you stand on the rope and pull upwards, make sure you have a sturdy pair of shoes.

Prepare for your exercise period with a brief warm-up (page 10). Doing a few jump-rope routines will help limber you up.

Never hold your breath while exercising, and stop immediately if you feel pain or dizziness.

That much said, take the following exercises one at a time, and have fun!

■ Arm Pull

Stand straight with your feet slightly apart. Hold the rope overhead, grasping the inside of the loop with your palms facing out. Avoid bending your arms at the elbows.

Spread your arms over your head, stretching the rope. Pull as hard as you can against the ends of the rope and hold that position. You'll feel the muscles in your arms, shoulders, and upper back tighten. After eight to ten seconds, release the rope. To loosen up, move your arms in wide circles from the shoulders.

■ Hand Pull

Adjust the rope until the loop is slightly wider than the width of your shoulders. Grasp the ends of the loop with your palms facing in. Pull your hands apart as hard as you can, stretching the rope. You'll feel your arm, shoulders, and back muscles contracting. Hold the position for eight to ten seconds and release.

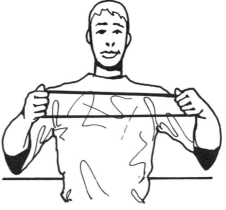

■ Reverse Arm Pull

Keep the loop slightly wider than your shoulders and grasp the ends of the loop with your palms facing out. Pull the loop as hard as you can, stretching the rope. Feel your shoulder, back, and arm muscles contracting. Release the pull after eight to ten seconds.

■ Chest Flex

Wrap the rope around your back, grasping it with your palms facing out. Push your hands straight out in front of you until you feel your chest, the front of your shoulders, and your upper arm muscles tighten. Hold the position for eight to ten seconds and release.

If the rope pulls against your back too forcefully, try wrapping a towel around your upper body.

■ Arm Curl

You may need to double over the rope for this one. Kneel down, securing one end of the loop against the ground with your knee. Grip the other end of the loop with your right hand, palm facing up. Raise your right hand, bending your right arm at the elbow. Make sure the rope

doesn't slip from under your knee. Hold the position for eight to ten seconds, flexing the biceps, lower arm muscles, shoulders, and upper back.

Reverse the procedure for the left arm.

■ Butterfly Lift

Stand straight with one end of the loop beneath your feet. Grasp the other end of the loop with both hands, palms down. Your hands should just touch each other. Bend the arms to the side to stretch the rope. The taut rope should reach just below your navel. Hold the position for eight to ten seconds before releasing. The Butterfly Lift works the muscles of your upper and lower back.

■ Straddle Lift

Stand on the rope with your feet spread apart. Grab the top of the loop with both hands placed close together, palms down. The rope should make a kind of triangle. Keep your back straight and bend your arms and legs slightly.

Pull upwards with your entire upper body, flexing the muscles of your legs, back, arms, shoulders, and midsection. Hold the position for eight to ten seconds and release.

■ **Power Lift**

Stand on the rope and spread your feet no wider than your shoulders. Grab the top of the loop with both hands placed together, palms down. Your hands should not touch. Bend your arms and knees and lean forward about 45 degrees.

Pull upwards, tightening the entire back, legs, buttocks, arms, and shoulders. Hold the position for eight to ten seconds and relax.

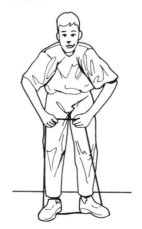

LEVELS OF DIFFICULTY AND STRESS

Like jogging, jumping rope impacts the ankles, knees, and hips. Good jumping form requires that you land on the balls of your feet, which provides excellent exercise for the calf muscles. However, it's best for individuals with chronic problems in these areas to avoid routines that stress them. Certain types of ankle sprains, for instance, can take a long time to heal. Even if you no longer experience discomfort in day-to-day activity, forcing yourself through twisting routines like Heels Out–Heels In or Crisscross Jumps may aggravate an old injury. Check the chart to see which routines make sense for you, and never continue a routine if you feel any pain or discomfort.

The repetitive wrist motions required to turn the rope may also lead to discomfort in some individuals. Spending many hours at computer keyboards has led to an increase in the nerve injury called Carpal Tunnel Syndrome. Any tenderness in the wrists should be taken very seriously.

If you're overweight, avoid routines that require high jumping or lots of ankle twisting. If you're a senior, or if you haven't exercised for the past three months, be careful about routines that stress the back, thighs, and ankles. Begin each routine slowly and perform it at a comfortable speed. Don't push or force yourself. Your body will tell you when you can speed things up.

Except for the Power Lift, which may stress the backs of some senior jumpers, anyone can do the isometric exercises (pages 88–92).

JUMPING ROUTINES AND GAMES

Easy. Slight stress on arches, ankles, calves, upper legs and knees.

Basic Jumping	Jumping to Music
Chinese Wheel	Rock the Cradle
Daisy Chain	Running the Gauntlet
Jumping Beans	Side Step
Jumping in a Row	Simple Hip Hop
Jumping Jacks	Tiny Kicks

Moderate. May require high jumps. Moderate stress on arches, ankles, calves, upper legs and knees.

Around the World	Running in Place
Charlie Chaplin	Side-by-Side and
Double Under	variations
Half Round	Skier
Heel Tap	Spoons
High Stepping	Squiggling Snake
High Tide	Switching Cousins
High Water, Low Water	Toe Tap
Irish Jig	Twister
Judo Jump	Two Loops
Jump and Duck	Umbrella
Keep On Truckin'	Visit and Switch
Kissin' Cousins	Visiting
Over the Waves	Visiting Cousins
Rainbow	

Difficult. May require very high jumps. Considerable stress on arches, ankles, calves, upper legs, knees and back.

Back-to-Back Eggbeater	Forward Eggbeater
Bent Over	Front Cross
Can-Can	Heel Click

Heels Out–Heels In
Jumping-Jack Scissors-Step
One-Leg Sideways Jump
Organ Pipes
Reverse Eggbeater
Right and Left
    Crisscross
Right and Left Turn Hops

Road Runner
Rocker
Scissors Step
Sun and Moon
Touch Jumps
Traveller
Triple Under

Difficult. Considerable stress on shoulders and elbows.

Behind the Back Cross
Bullfighter
Front to Back Cross
Pretzel

Difficult. Considerable stress on back and legs.

Circle of Poison

NON-JUMPING ROUTINES

Easy. Slight stress on shoulders, elbows and wrists.

Arm Curl
Arm Pull
Butterfly Lift
Chest Flex
Figure Eights

Hand Pull
Reverse Arm Pull
Straddle Lift
Waist Wrap

Moderate. More stress on shoulders and elbows, stress on upper legs.

Bolas
Leg Over Eights
Open Waist Wrap

Power Lift
Samurai Warrior
Shoulder Wrap

INDEX